Easy Lemonade Cookbook

Delicious Lemonade Recipes for Every Season and Occasion

By
BookSumo Press
All rights reserved

Published by
http://www.booksumo.com

ENJOY THE RECIPES?
KEEP ON COOKING WITH 6 MORE FREE COOKBOOKS!

Visit our website and simply enter your email address to join the club and receive your 6 cookbooks.

http://booksumo.com/magnet

https://www.instagram.com/booksumopress/

https://www.facebook.com/booksumo/

LEGAL NOTES

All Rights Reserved. No Part Of This Book May Be Reproduced Or Transmitted In Any Form Or By Any Means. Photocopying, Posting Online, And / Or Digital Copying Is Strictly Prohibited Unless Written Permission Is Granted By The Book's Publishing Company. Limited Use Of The Book's Text Is Permitted For Use In Reviews Written For The Public.

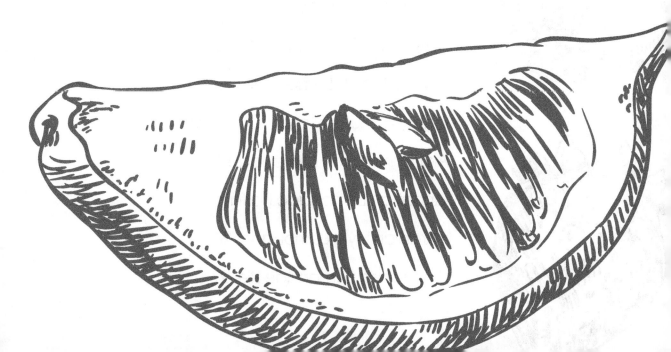

Table of Contents

Harvest Moon Lemonade 9

Animal Crossing Lemonade 10

Lemonade Ontario 11

Lemonade Summers 12

Lime-onade 13

Pennsylvanian Country Lemonade 14

Caitlyn's Cupcake Lemonaded 15

Garden Lemonade Dip 16

Brooklyn Strawberry Lemonade 17

Lemonade Cheesecake 18

Vanilla Lemonade Ice Cream Pie 19

Backroad Lemonade 20

4-Ingredient Lemonade Pie 21

More Melon Lemonade 22

Meghan's Muffins Lemonaded 23

Alabama Porch Lemonade 24

Manhattan Lemonade Parfaits 25

Arabian Style Lemonade 26

Tennessee Lemonade Pie 27

Mediterranean Lemonade 28

Apricot Pineapple Lemonade 29

Hawaiian Lemonade Pie 30

Georgia Lemonade 31

Sandy's Scones Lemonaded 32

Lime and Mango Lemonade 33

Persian Lemonade 34

English Brewed Lemonade 35

2-Berry Lemonade 36

North Carolina Style Lemonade 37

Country Fruit Lemonade 38

Caribbean Style Lemonade 39

Spring Time Lemonade 40

Lemonade Cake 41

Black Tea lemonade 42

Early Autumn Lemonade 43

Persian Lemonade II 44

Virginia State Lemonade 45

Orange Lemonade 46

Deep Lemonade 47

4th Grade Lemonade 48

Mandy's Mango Lemonade 49

3-Ingredient Lemonade-Tea 50

New Lemonade Technology Tea 51

Lemonade Tunisian 52

French Lemonade 53

College Lemonade 54

Cupcakes-Limon 55

Lemonade Levantine 57

Rio De Janeiro Restaurant Lemonade 58

Heirloom Kitchen Lemonade 59

Summer Solstice Lemonade 60

Lemonade Madras 61

Lemonade in France 62

Lena's Lemonade 63

Lemonade in France 64

Mexican Lemonade 65

Lemonade for Lovers 66

Lunch Truck Lemonade 67

Red Lemonade 68

Lemonade Icee's 69

Arizona Mesa Lemonade 70

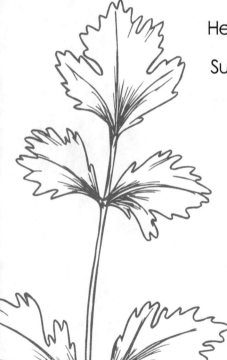

Rachela's Sweet Lemonade with Vegetable Syrup 71

Greek Lemonade 72

Festival Lemonade 73

Vietnamese Lemonade 74

Israeli Style Lemonade 75

October Cinnamon Clove Lemonade 76

Tarrytown Lemonade 77

Sanibel Island Lemonade 78

Hawaiian Lemonade 79

Lemonade Lake 80

Root Lemonade 81

Lemonade Pagani 82

Leafy Lemonade 83

London Lemonade Squares 84

Canadian Mexican Lemonade 85

Rosemary Honey Lemonade 86

Mother's Day Lemonade 87

Lemonade in Vietcong 88

Sweet Basil Lemonade 89

Lemonade Monday Muffins 90

Dade County Lemonade 91

How to Make Lemonade Syrup 92

Cucumber Lemonade 93

Toddler's Lemonade 94

Hawaiian Tribal Lemonade 95

State Fair Lemonade 96

Urban Garden Lemonade 97

Lemonade Saint Kitts 98

Lebanese Lemonade 99

Black Lemonade 100

Harvest Moon Lemonade

Prep Time: 15 mins
Total Time: 15 mins

Servings per Recipe: 4
Calories	138.9
Fat	0.3g
Cholesterol	0.0mg
Sodium	5.1mg
Carbohydrates	35.7g
Protein	1.0g

Ingredients

- 1 C. water
- 1/2 C. granulated sugar
- 1/2 C. fresh mint leaves, packed
- 3 kiwi fruits, peeled and cut into chunks
- 2 - 3 lemons, juiced
- sparkling water

Directions

1. Place the sugar and water in a pot over medium-high heat and cook until sugar dissolves completely, stirring often.
2. Now, set the heat to low and cook for about 4 minutes, mixing time to time.
3. Remove from the heat and immediately, mix the mint leaves.
4. Keep aside for about 20 minutes.
5. In a blender, add the kiwifruit and pulse until pureed.
6. In a pitcher, place the pureed kiwi.
7. Through a strainer, strain the cooled syrup into the pitcher, pressing with the back of a spoon.
8. Place the pitcher in fridge to chill.
9. Add the lemon juice and stir to combine.
10. Transfer into serving glasses and enjoy with a garnishing of the kiwi slices.

ANIMAL CROSSING
Lemonade

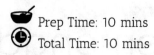

Prep Time: 10 mins
Total Time: 10 mins

Servings per Recipe: 8
Calories   127.9
Fat   0.1g
Cholesterol   0.0mg
Sodium   1.2mg
Carbohydrates   35.1g
Protein   0.9g

Ingredients

3 oranges
3 lemons
1 lime

1 C. sugar
water

Directions

1. In a bowl, extract the juice of lime, lemons and oranges.
2. In a pitcher, add the sugar, citrus juice and enough water to make 8 cups of drink and stir until sugar is dissolved.
3. Transfer into ice filled glasses and enjoy.

Lemonade Ontario

🥣 Prep Time: 1 min
🕐 Total Time: 1 min

Servings per Recipe: 1	
Calories	0.0
Fat	0.0g
Cholesterol	0.0mg
Sodium	20.5mg
Carbohydrates	0.0g
Protein	0.0g

Ingredients

3 (4 g) packets of crystal light lemonade
3 (12 oz.) cans of fizzy water
basil leaves, torn
fresh ginger, grated

Directions

1. In a pitcher, add all the ingredients and mix well.
2. Transfer into ice filled glasses and enjoy.

LEMONADE
Summers

Prep Time: 15 mins
Total Time: 15 mins

Servings per Recipe: 12
Calories 173.4
Fat 0.6g
Cholesterol 0.0mg
Sodium 8.4mg
Carbohydrates 44.0g
Protein 0.7g

Ingredients

8 C. cubed seedless watermelon
2 (12 oz.) cans frozen lemonade concentrate
4 C. water

Directions

1. In a food processor, add the watermelon and pulse until pureed.
2. In a pitcher, add water, pureed watermelon and lemonade concentrate and with a long wooden spoon, stir to combine well.
3. Enjoy with a garnishing of the extra watermelon.

Lime-onade

🥣 Prep Time: 10 mins
🕐 Total Time: 10 mins

Servings per Recipe: 1	
Calories	109.0
Fat	0.0g
Cholesterol	0.0mg
Sodium	5.7mg
Carbohydrates	29.0g
Protein	0.2g

Ingredients

1/2 C. fresh lime juice
1/2 C. fresh lemon juice
3/4 C. sugar
4 C. cold water

1 lemon, sliced
ice cube

Directions

1. Place the sugar, lemon and lime juice in a pitcher and with a long wooden spoon, stir until sugar is dissolved completely.
2. Stir in the remaining ingredients and until combined nicely.
3. Enjoy.

PENNSYLVANIAN Country Lemonade

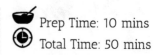

Prep Time: 10 mins
Total Time: 50 mins

Servings per Recipe: 4
Calories 102.0
Fat 0.0g
Cholesterol 0.0mg
Sodium 7.6mg
Carbohydrates 27.7g
Protein 0.4g

Ingredients

1/2 C. packed chopped mint leaves
1/3 C. chopped fresh ginger
1/3 C. honey
2 C. boiling water
1/2 C. fresh lemon juice
1 1/2 C. cold water

Toppings
ice cube
fresh mint leaves
lemon slice

Directions

1. In a bowl, honey, ginger and, chopped mint and boiling water and stir to combine well.
2. Keep aside for about 35-40 minutes.
3. Through a strainer, strain the mixture into a pitcher, pressing with the back of a spoon to extract liquid.
4. Add the cold water and lemon juice and mix well.
5. Transfer into ice filled glasses and enjoy with a garnishing of the fresh lemon slices and mint leaves.

Caitlyn's Cupcake Lemonaded

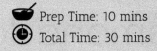
Prep Time: 10 mins
Total Time: 30 mins

Servings per Recipe: 1	
Calories	209.5
Fat	8.6g
Cholesterol	32.3mg
Sodium	200.2mg
Carbohydrates	31.5g
Protein	2.2g

Ingredients

- 1 (6 oz.) cans frozen lemonade concentrate, thawed
- 1 (18 1/4 oz.) boxes white cake mix
- 1 (8 oz.) cartons sour cream
- 3 oz. cream cheese, softened
- 3 eggs
- 1 (12 oz.) cans whipped cream cheese frosting

Directions

1. Set your oven to 350 degrees F before doing anything else and line cups of muffin pans with the paper liners.
2. Discard about 2 tbsp of the lemonade concentrate from can.
3. In a bowl, add the cake mix, eggs, cream cheese, sour cream and remaining concentrate and with an electric mixer, beat until well combined.
4. Place the mixture into prepared muffin cups about 3/4 of the full.
5. Cook in the oven for about 20 minutes or until a toothpick inserted in the center comes out clean.
6. Remove from the oven and keep onto the wire rack to cool in the pan for about 5-10 minutes.
7. Carefully, invert the muffins onto the wire rack to cool completely.
8. Spread the frosting over cooled muffins and enjoy.

GARDEN Lemonade Dip

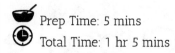

Prep Time: 5 mins
Total Time: 1 hr 5 mins

Servings per Recipe:	12
Calories	9.0
Fat	0.1g
Cholesterol	0.7mg
Sodium	51.5mg
Carbohydrates	0.5g
Protein	1.3g

Ingredients

4 oz. fat free cream cheese
1 tsp pink sugar-free lemonade-flavored drink mix
1 1/2 C. fat-free cool whip

Directions

1. In a bowl, add the lemonade mix and cream cheese and beat until well blended and smooth.
2. Add 1/2 C. of the Cool Whip and beat until well blended.
3. Gently, fold in the remaining Cool Whip.
4. Place the bowl in fridge for about 1 1/2-2 hours.
5. Enjoy with your favorite fruit slices.

Brooklyn Strawberry Lemonade

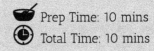

Prep Time: 10 mins
Total Time: 10 mins

Servings per Recipe: 8
Calories	100.6
Fat	0.2g
Cholesterol	0.0mg
Sodium	16.2mg
Carbohydrates	25.8g
Protein	0.5g

Ingredients

3 C. water, cold
1 quart strawberries
3/4 C. sugar
3/4 C. lemon juice
2 C. club soda, cold
lemon slice

Directions

1. In a food processor, add the sugar, strawberries and water and pulse until smooth.
2. Transfer the strawberry mixture into a pitcher.
3. Add the lemon juice and soda and with a long wooden spoon, stir to combine.
4. Enjoy with a garnishing of the lemon slices.

LEMONADE
Cheesecake

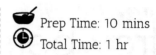

Prep Time: 10 mins
Total Time: 1 hr

Servings per Recipe: 10
Calories   4388.1
Fat   191.4g
Cholesterol   890.9mg
Sodium   4283.8mg
Carbohydrates   624.5g
Protein   56.9g

Ingredients

Cake
1 (18 oz.) packages white cake mix
1 C. sour cream
3 oz. cream cheese, softened
3 eggs
6 oz. lemonade concentrate, thawed

Frosting
1 C. sour cream
1 C. powdered sugar
1 tbsp lemon juice

Directions

1. Set your oven to 350 degrees F before doing anything else and grease and flour a Bundt pan.
2. For the cake: in a bowl, add all the ingredients and with an electric mixer, beat on high speed until well combined.
3. Transfer the mixture into the prepared Bundt pan evenly.
4. Cook in the oven for about 50-60 minutes.
5. Remove from the oven and keep onto the wire rack to cool in the pan for about 10 minutes.
6. Carefully, invert the cake onto the wire rack to cool completely.
7. Meanwhile, for the glaze: in a bowl, add all the ingredients and beat until smooth.
8. Place the glaze on the top of cooled cake and enjoy.

Vanilla Lemonade Ice Cream Pie

Prep Time: 10 mins
Total Time: 10 mins

Servings per Recipe: 10
Calories   230.5
Fat   13.8g
Cholesterol   11.6mg
Sodium   147.0mg
Carbohydrates   25.1g
Protein   2.0g

Ingredients

1/3 C. country time lemonade mix
1/2 C. water
1 pint vanilla ice cream
1 (8 oz.) containers Cool Whip
1 (9 oz.) graham cracker pie crust

Directions

1. In a pitcher, add the lemonade and water and with a long wooden spoon, stir to combine well.
2. Add the ice cream and with the soon, mix until smooth.
3. Now, place the Cool Whip and mix until well blended.
4. In a prepared pie crust, place the lemonade mixture and place in the freeze for about 5 hours.

BACKROAD
Lemonade

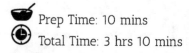
Prep Time: 10 mins
Total Time: 3 hrs 10 mins

Servings per Recipe: 6
Calories   121.6
Fat   0.0g
Cholesterol   0.0mg
Sodium   7.0mg
Carbohydrates   32.1g
Protein   0.4g

Ingredients

1 C. loose-packed fresh mint leaves
2/3 C. sugar
1 C. fresh lemon juice
3 C. water
1 C. canned peach nectar, chilled

peach slices
fresh mint sprig

Directions

1. In a glass bowl, add the sugar and mint and with the back of a spoon, crush the leaves.
2. Add the water and lemon juice and stir until sugar dissolves completely.
3. Through a fine mesh strainer, strain the mixture into a pitcher.
4. Add the peach nectar and mix well.
5. Refrigerate, covered to chill for about 6 hours.
6. Transfer into ice filled glasses and enjoy with a garnishing of the peach slices and mint sprigs.

4-Ingredient Lemonade Pie

🥣 Prep Time: 10 mins
🕐 Total Time: 24 hrs 10 mins

Servings per Recipe: 8	
Calories	441.0
Fat	19.0g
Cholesterol	16.8mg
Sodium	242.4mg
Carbohydrates	64.2g
Protein	5.5g

Ingredients

1 (6 oz.) cans frozen lemonade
1 (14 oz.) cans sweetened condensed milk
1 (8 oz.) containers Cool Whip

1 graham cracker crust

Directions

1. In a bowl, add the frozen lemonade, condensed milk and Cool Whip and with an electric mixer, beat until fluffy.
2. In a prepared pie crust, place the lemonade mixture and place in the fridge for the whole night.

MORE MELON Lemonade

Prep Time: 25 mins
Total Time: 24 hrs 25 mins

Servings per Recipe: 12
Calories 185.0
Fat 0.7g
Cholesterol 0.0mg
Sodium 11.2mg
Carbohydrates 46.8g
Protein 1.0g

Ingredients

8 C. cubed seeded watermelon
3 C. hulled and quartered strawberries
2 (12 oz.) cans frozen lemonade concentrate, thawed
8 C. water

wedges of fresh watermelon
whole hulled strawberry

Directions

1. In a food processor, add the strawberries, watermelon and lemonade concentrate in 2 batches and pulse until smooth.
2. Transfer the mixture into a container with the water and mix well.
3. Refrigerate for about 2-3 days.
4. Transfer into ice filled glasses and enjoy with a garnishing of the strawberries and watermelon wedges.
5. Makes 12 servings.
6. Make-Ahead.
7. Make up to 2 days ahead; cover and refrigerate. To serve, stir and add berries and watermelon wedges.

Meghan's Muffins Lemonaded

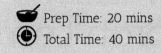
Prep Time: 20 mins
Total Time: 40 mins

Servings per Recipe: 1
Calories   292.9
Fat   15.0g
Cholesterol   27.5mg
Sodium   272.8mg
Carbohydrates   36.4g
Protein   4.6g

Ingredients

1 1/2 C. flour
1/4 C. sugar
2 1/2 tsp baking powder
1/2 tsp salt
1 beaten egg
1 (6 oz.) cans frozen lemonade, thawed
1/4 C. milk
1/3 C. cooking oil
1/2 C. chopped walnuts

Directions

1. Set your oven to 375 degrees F before doing anything else and grease 8-9 cups of a large muffin pan.
2. In a bowl, add the flour, sugar, baking powder and salt and mix well.
3. In a separate bowl, add the milk, oil, egg and 1/2 C. of the lemonade and beat until well combined.
4. Add the egg mixture into the flour mixture and mix until just combined.
5. Fold in the walnuts.
6. Transfer the mixture into the prepared muffin cups evenly.
7. Cook in the oven for about 15-20 minutes or until a toothpick inserted in the center comes out clean.
8. Remove from the oven and keep onto the wire rack to cool in the pan for about 5 minutes.
9. Carefully, invert the muffins onto the wire rack.
10. Coat the muffins with the remaining lemonade evenly.
11. Enjoy with the du

ALABAMA
Porch Lemonade

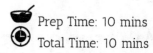

Prep Time: 10 mins
Total Time: 10 mins

Servings per Recipe: 4
Calories   45.6
Fat   0.0g
Cholesterol   0.0mg
Sodium   5.2mg
Carbohydrates   12.3g
Protein   0.2g

Ingredients

1/2 C. rinsed lightly packed basil leaf
3 tbsp sugar
4 C. water

1/2 C. squeezed lemon juice
1 sprig basil

Directions

1. In a large non-metallic bowl, add the sugar and basil leaves and crush the leaves with a wooden spoon until bruised completely.
2. Add the lemon juice and water and mix until sugar dissolves completely.
3. Through a fine mesh strainer, strain the mixture into glasses of ice.
4. Enjoy with a garnishing of the fresh basil sprigs.

Manhattan Lemonade Parfaits

Prep Time: 5 mins
Total Time: 2 hrs 5 mins

Servings per Recipe: 4
Calories 440.1
Fat 26.3g
Cholesterol 29.0mg
Sodium 122.0mg
Carbohydrates 46.1g
Protein 6.1g

Ingredients

- 1/2 C. graham cracker crumbs
- 1/2 C. granola cereal
- 1/3 C. country time lemonade mix
- 1/2 C. water
- 1 pint vanilla ice cream, softened
- 8 oz. Cool Whip
- 1 lemon, wedges

Directions

1. In a blender, add the granola and cracker crumbs and process until a crumbly mixture is formed.
2. Transfer the crumbly mixture into a bowl and keep aside.
3. In a bowl, add the water and lemonade mix and mix until well combined.
4. In another bowl, add the ice cream and lemonade mixture and with an electric mixer, beat on low speed until well combined.
5. Add the whipped topping and gently, stir to combine.
6. Divide the crumbs mixture in 4 parfait glasses evenly, followed by half of the lemonade mixture.
7. Repeat the layers once.
8. Place the parfait glasses in freezer for about 2 1/2 - 3 hours.
9. Enjoy with a garnishing of the lemon slices.

ARABIAN STYLE
Lemonade

Prep Time: 10 mins
Total Time: 10 mins

Servings per Recipe: 6
Calories   120.8
Fat   0.2g
Cholesterol   0.0mg
Sodium   7.6mg
Carbohydrates   32.5g
Protein   0.9g

Ingredients

8 lemons, juiced
3/4 C. sugar
1/4 C. mint
4 C. water
ice cube

Directions

1. In a large non-metallic bowl, add the sugar and mint leaves and crush the mint with a wooden spoon until bruised completely.
2. Add the lemon juice and water and mix until well combined.
3. Transfer into ice filled glasses and enjoy.

Tennessee Lemonade Pie

Prep Time: 10 mins
Total Time: 10 mins

Servings per Recipe: 8
Calories	425.5
Fat	16.9g
Cholesterol	16.8mg
Sodium	195.0mg
Carbohydrates	65.5g
Protein	5.2g

Ingredients

14 oz. sweetened condensed milk
6 oz. frozen lemonade concentrate, thawed
3 tbsp seedless raspberry preserves
8 oz. frozen whipped topping, thawed
6 oz. prepared graham cracker crusts

Directions

1. In a bowl, add the condensed milk, lemonade concentrate and raspberry preserves and beat until smooth.
2. Add the whipped topping and gently, stir to combine.
3. In the prepared crust, lace the mixture and place in freezer for about 5 hours.
4. Enjoy with a garnishing of the raspberries and fresh mint.

MEDITERRANEAN
Lemonade

Prep Time: 10 mins
Total Time: 10 mins

Servings per Recipe: 6
Calories	70.3
Fat	0.0g
Cholesterol	0.0mg
Sodium	3.3mg
Carbohydrates	18.5g
Protein	0.1g

Ingredients

1/2 C. fresh lemon juice
1/2 C. sugar
1/4 C. fresh mint leaves
2 C. water
3 C. ice cubes

Directions

1. In a food processor, add the sugar, mint leaves and lemons and pulse until chopped.
2. Add the ice and water and pulse until smooth.
3. Transfer into serving glasses and enjoy.

Apricot Pineapple Lemonade

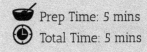

Prep Time: 5 mins
Total Time: 5 mins

Servings per Recipe: 6	
Calories	148.7
Fat	0.2g
Cholesterol	0.0mg
Sodium	8.6mg
Carbohydrates	38.0g
Protein	0.5g

Ingredients

6 oz. cans frozen lemonade concentrate, thawed
3/4 C. water
1 (12 oz.) cans apricot nectar, chilled
1 (12 oz.) cans unsweetened pineapple juice, chilled
ice cube
1 1/4 C. ginger ale, chilled
lemon slice

Directions

1. Place the water and lemonade concentrate in a pitcher and with a long wooden spoon, stir to combine well.
2. Add the pineapple juice and apricot nectar and mix until well combined.
3. Add the lemon slices, ginger ale and ice cubes and stir to combine.
4. Enjoy.

HAWAIIAN
Lemonade Pie

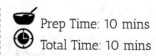

Prep Time: 10 mins
Total Time: 10 mins

Servings per Recipe: 6
Calories   627.0
Fat   24.4g
Cholesterol   17.3mg
Sodium   305.0mg
Carbohydrates   99.6g
Protein   6.3g

Ingredients

1 (16 oz.) cans frozen pink lemonade concentrate, thawed
1 C. sweetened condensed milk

1 (8 oz.) cartons Cool Whip
1 (9 inch) graham cracker crust

Directions

1. In a bowl, add all the ingredients except the pie crust and mix until smooth.
2. Place the mixture into the prepared pie shell and freeze overnight.

Georgia Lemonade

Prep Time: 10 mins
Total Time: 20 mins

Servings per Recipe: 4	
Calories	224.0
Fat	0.1g
Cholesterol	0.0mg
Sodium	5.2mg
Carbohydrates	58.6g
Protein	0.6g

Ingredients

2 peaches, peeled and chopped
1 C. granulated sugar
4 C. water
3/4 C. squeezed lemon juice

mint sprig
peach slices

Directions

1. In a pan, add the sugar, peaches and water and cook until boiling.
2. Now, set the heat to low and cook for about 10 minutes, stirring frequently.
3. Remove from the heat and keep aside to cool completely.
4. Through a fine mesh strainer, strain the mixture into a pitcher, pressing with the back of a spoon to extract all the juice.
5. Add the lemon juice and stir to combine well.
6. Transfer into serving ice filled glasses evenly.
7. Enjoy with a garnishing of the mint and peach slices.

SANDY'S Scones Lemonaded

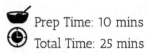

Prep Time: 10 mins
Total Time: 25 mins

Servings per Recipe: 8
Calories 280.9
Fat 11.4g
Cholesterol 40.7mg
Sodium 627.2mg
Carbohydrates 38.8g
Protein 5.2g

Ingredients

1 C. heavy cream
1 C. lemonade
3 C. self-raising flour
1 pinch salt
jam
cream

Directions

1. Set your oven to 450 degrees F before doing anything else and grease a baking sheet.
2. In a bowl, add all the ingredients and gently, mix until well blended.
3. Place the dough onto a floured surface and with your hands; knead for 2-3 times.
4. Roll the dough into 1-inch thickness.
5. With a round cutter, cut the scones.
6. In the prepared baking sheet, arrange the scones in a single layer.
7. Coat the top of each scone with some milk.
8. Cook in the oven for about 10-15 minutes.
9. Enjoy alongside the cream and jam.

Lime and Mango Lemonade

Prep Time: 10 mins
Total Time: 15 mins

Servings per Recipe: 1
Calories   703.1
Fat   0.4g
Cholesterol   0.0mg
Sodium   16.3mg
Carbohydrates   183.2g
Protein   1.1g

Ingredients

2 C. chopped mangoes, pureed
5 C. cold water
1/2 C. fresh lime juice

1 1/2 C. sugar

Directions

1. In a pitcher, add the dissolved sugar, mango puree and water and mix well.
2. Add the lime juice and stir to combine.
3. Transfer into ice filled glasses and enjoy.

PERSIAN
Lemonade

Prep Time: 5 mins
Total Time: 1 hr 5 mins

Servings per Recipe: 6
Calories	142.5
Fat	0.0g
Cholesterol	0.0mg
Sodium	4.7mg
Carbohydrates	38.0g
Protein	0.2g

Ingredients

5 1/3 C. water
1 C. granulated sugar
1 1/3 C. fresh lemon juice
2 1/2-3 1/2 tsp rose water

Directions

1. In a pan, add the sugar and water over medium-low heat and cook until sugar dissolves, stirring continuously.
2. Remove from the heat and keep aside to cool completely.
3. Transfer the cooled sugar syrup into a pitcher with the lemon juice and rose water and mix well.
4. Place in the fridge to chill completely.
5. Enjoy chilled.

English Brewed Lemonade

Prep Time: 5 mins
Total Time: 5 mins

Servings per Recipe: 4
Calories   82.2
Fat   0.1g
Cholesterol   0.0mg
Sodium   8.7mg
Carbohydrates   23.0g
Protein   0.3g

Ingredients

4 C. brewed green tea
1 C. fresh lemon juice
1/4 C. honey

ice
4 lemon wedges

Directions

1. Add all the ingredients except the ice into a pitcher and with a long wooden spoon, stir to combine.
2. Stir in the ice and enjoy.

2-BERRY Lemonade

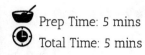

Prep Time: 5 mins
Total Time: 5 mins

Servings per Recipe: 1
Calories   98.1
Fat   0.4g
Cholesterol   0.0mg
Sodium   6.2mg
Carbohydrates   25.8g
Protein   1.2g

Ingredients

1/2 kiwi
3 medium strawberries
1 lemon
1/2 C. water

1 - 1 1/2 tbsp sugar
2 ice cubes

Directions

1. With your hands, squeeze the strawberries and kiwi into bowl.
2. Squeeze the lemons in the bowl with a lemon squeezer.
3. Add the sugar and water and stir until sugar is dissolved.
4. Enjoy.

North Carolina Style Lemonade

Prep Time: 20 mins
Total Time: 20 mins

Servings per Recipe: 1
Calories   114.7
Fat   0.2g
Cholesterol   0.0mg
Sodium   3.8mg
Carbohydrates   29.7g
Protein   0.4g

Ingredients

- 1/3 C. fresh lemon juice
- 2 C. water
- 2 C. fresh blueberries
- 1/2 C. sugar

Directions

1. In a food processor, add all the ingredients and pulse until smooth.
2. With a fine mesh strainer, strain the mixture into a pitcher.
3. Transfer into ice filled glasses and enjoy.

COUNTRY FRUIT
Lemonade

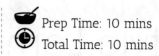

Prep Time: 10 mins
Total Time: 10 mins

Servings per Recipe: 1
Calories	685.3
Fat	2.0g
Cholesterol	0.0mg
Sodium	139.3mg
Carbohydrates	174.4g
Protein	1.6g

Ingredients

2 (12 oz.) cans frozen lemonade concentrate, thawed
2 (10 oz.) packages frozen sweetened raspberries, thawed
2 - 4 tbsp sugar
2 liters club soda, chilled
ice cube

Directions

1. In a food processor, add the sugar, raspberries and lemonade concentrate and pulse until well combined.
2. Through a strainer, strain the mixture, pressing with the back of a spoon.
3. In a large pitcher, add the club soda, raspberry mixture and ice cubes and stir to combine well.
4. Enjoy.

Caribbean Style Lemonade

Prep Time: 10 mins
Total Time: 15 mins

Servings per Recipe: 8
Calories	124.8
Fat	0.0g
Cholesterol	0.0mg
Sodium	4.5mg
Carbohydrates	32.7g
Protein	0.4g

Ingredients

- 1 C. sugar
- 1 C. boiling water
- 3 1/2 C. cold water, divided
- 3 C. peeled chopped papayas
- 1 C. fresh lemon juice

Directions

1. In a bowl, add the boiling water and sugar and mix until sugar is dissolved completely.
2. Keep aside to cool for about 4-5 minutes.
3. In a food processor, add the papaya, sugar syrup, lemon juice and 2 C. of the cold water and pulse until smooth.
4. Transfer the mixture into a pitcher with the remaining cold water and stir to combine.
5. Transfer into ice filled glasses and enjoy.

SPRING TIME
Lemonade

Prep Time: 5 mins
Total Time: 10 mins

Servings per Recipe: 6
Calories   73.9
Fat   0.1g
Cholesterol   0.0mg
Sodium   11.3mg
Carbohydrates   19.6g
Protein   0.1g

Ingredients

6 jasmine green tea bags
1/2-1 C. sugar
1 tbsp lemon zest
9 C. filtered water
1 C. fresh lemon juice

Garnish
jasmine fresh edible flower
fresh lemon rind
mint leaf

Directions

1. In the reserve of the coffee maker, add the water.
2. Put the unbleached filter in the coffee filter.
3. Add the sugar, tea bags and lemon zest and process until sugar is dissolved.
4. Transfer the tea into a pitcher and keep aside to cool completely.
5. Add the lemon juice and stir to combine.
6. Add enough ice cubes to fill the pitcher.
7. Transfer into ice filled glasses and enjoy with a garnishing of the jasmine flower, lemon rind or mint leaves.

Lemonade Cake

Prep Time: 8 mins
Total Time: 1 hr 3 mins

Servings per Recipe: 10	
Calories	339.8
Fat	12.3g
Cholesterol	75.2mg
Sodium	432.8mg
Carbohydrates	53.3g
Protein	4.3g

Ingredients

- 1 (15 oz.) packages yellow cake mix
- 1 (3 oz.) packages Jell-O vanilla
- 4 oz. country time lemonade mix, divided
- 1 C. cold water
- 4 eggs
- 1/4 C. oil
- 3 tbsp warm water
- 1 C. powdered sugar

Directions

1. Set your oven to 350 degrees F before doing anything else and grease and flour a fluted tube pan.
2. In a bowl, add the 1/4 C. of the drink mix, pudding mix, cake mix, oil, eggs and 1 C. of the water and with an electric mixer, beat on low speed for about 1 minute.
3. Now, set the mixer on medium speed and beat for about 4 minutes.
4. Transfer the mixture into the prepared tube pan evenly.
5. Cook in the oven for about 50-55 minutes or until a toothpick inserted in the center comes out clean.
6. Remove from the oven and keep onto the wire rack to cool in the pan for about 10 minutes.
7. Carefully, invert the cake onto a platter.
8. Meanwhile, for the glaze: in a bowl, add the remaining 1/4 C. of the drink and 3 tbsp of the warm water and mix until well combined.
9. Add the powdered sugar and beat until well combined.
10. With a fork, poke the warm cake at many places about 1-inch apart.
11. Place the glaze over the warm cake and keep aside until glaze absorbs completely.

BLACK TEA
Lemonade

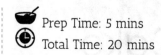
Prep Time: 5 mins
Total Time: 20 mins

Servings per Recipe: 4
Calories	42.1
Fat	0.0g
Cholesterol	0.0mg
Sodium	0.6mg
Carbohydrates	11.4g
Protein	0.8g

Ingredients

3/4 C. Splenda granular
1 tbsp grated fresh ginger root
12 allspice berries
8 whole cloves
4 black tea bags

2/3 C. lemon juice
2 unpeeled oranges, sliced

Directions

1. In a pot, add the 1 C. of water, ginger root, sugar, allspice and cloves over medium heat and cook until boiling, stirring continuously.
2. Set the heat to low and cook for about 4-5 minutes.
3. Remove from the heat and stir in the teabags.
4. Keep aside, covered for about 6 minutes.
5. Through a fine mesh strainer, strain into a pitcher.
6. Add the orange juice, lemon juice and 3 C. of the cold water and with the back of a spoon, crush the oranges slightly.
7. Transfer into ice filled glasses and enjoy.

Early Autumn Lemonade

Prep Time: 15 mins
Total Time: 15 mins

Servings per Recipe: 6
Calories	191.6
Fat	0.3g
Cholesterol	0.0mg
Sodium	8.6mg
Carbohydrates	51.2g
Protein	1.1g

Ingredients

- 10 -12 medium lemons, scrubbed well, halved
- 3 tbsp grated fresh ginger
- 1 1/4 C. granulated sugar
- 1 pinch salt
- 5 C. cold water

Directions

1. In a bowl, add the sugar, salt, ginger and lemons and with a wooden spoon, crush for about 5 minutes.
2. Through a strainer, strain the syrup and lemon slices in 2 batches, pressing with the back of a spoon.
3. In a pitcher, add the lemon mixture and water and mix well.
4. Refrigerate until chilled completely.
5. Transfer into ice filled glasses and enjoy.

PERSIAN Lemonade II

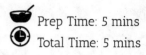

Prep Time: 5 mins
Total Time: 5 mins

Servings per Recipe: 1
Calories   88.2
Fat   0.2g
Cholesterol   0.0mg
Sodium   9.6mg
Carbohydrates   25.1g
Protein   0.9g

Ingredients

1 C. water
1 large lemon, juiced
1 tbsp honey

1 small dashes orange blossom water

Directions

1. In a pitcher, add all the ingredients and mix until well combined.
2. Refrigerate until chilled completely.
3. Transfer into ice filled glasses and enjoy.

Virginia State Lemonade

Prep Time: 15 mins
Total Time: 17 mins

Servings per Recipe: 1	
Calories	599.8
Fat	0.4g
Cholesterol	0.0mg
Sodium	15.4mg
Carbohydrates	157.2g
Protein	2.0g

Ingredients

- 4 C. water
- 1 C. sugar
- 1 C. lemon juice
- 1 tbsp grated lemon peel
- 1 C. blackberry
- 1 - 2 drop blue food coloring

Directions

1. In a pan, add the sugar and 2 C. of the water and cook until boiling, mixing frequently.
2. Cook for about 3 minutes.
3. Remove from the heat and stir in the lemon peel, lemon juice and remaining 2 C. of the water.
4. Keep aside to cool for some time.
5. In a food processor, add the blackberries and 1 C. of the lemon mixture and pulse until well combined.
6. Through a strainer, strain the mixture into a pitcher.
7. In a pitcher, add the blackberries and remaining lemon mixture and food coloring and stir to combine well.
8. Refrigerate until chilled completely.
9. Transfer into ice filled glasses and enjoy.

ORANGE Lemonade

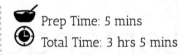

Prep Time: 5 mins
Total Time: 3 hrs 5 mins

Servings per Recipe: 8
Calories 108.8
Fat 0.3g
Cholesterol 0.0mg
Sodium 6.5mg
Carbohydrates 27.3g
Protein 0.1g

Ingredients

3 tea bags tag and string removed
3 C. boiling water
1 (12 oz.) cans frozen lemonade concentrate
1 tsp orange extract

Directions

1. In a pitcher, add the water and tea bags and keep aside, covered for about 12-15 minutes.
2. Add the orange extract and lemonade concentrate and mix well.
3. Add enough cold water to fill the pitcher.
4. Refrigerate for about 4-5 hours.
5. Transfer into ice filled glasses and enjoy.

Deep Lemonade

Prep Time: 10 mins
Total Time: 10 mins

Servings per Recipe: 10
Calories	87.2
Fat	0.0g
Cholesterol	0.0mg
Sodium	6.1mg
Carbohydrates	22.4g
Protein	0.1g

Ingredients

- 8 C. water
- 1 C. sugar
- 2 blood oranges, juice
- 2 lemons, juice
- 1 tsp orange blossom water

Directions

1. In a pitcher, add the sugar and water and mix until sugar is dissolved.
2. Add orange juice, lemon juice and blossom water and mix well.
3. Refrigerate to chill completely.
4. Transfer into ice filled glasses and enjoy.

4TH GRADE
Lemonade

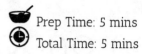

Prep Time: 5 mins
Total Time: 5 mins

Servings per Recipe: 1
Calories　　　　1763.6
Fat　　　　　　14.8g
Cholesterol　　　3.0mg
Sodium　　　　553.1mg
Carbohydrates　416.1g
Protein　　　　9.0g

Ingredients

1 (12 oz.) cans lemonade concentrate
water
1/4 C. chocolate syrup

Directions

1. In a pitcher, add the water and lemonade concentrate and mix well.
2. Add the chocolate syrup and stir to combine well.
3. Transfer into ice filled glasses and enjoy.

Mandy's Mango Lemonade

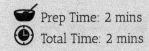

Prep Time: 2 mins
Total Time: 2 mins

Servings per Recipe: 4	
Calories	291.6
Fat	1.3g
Cholesterol	0.0mg
Sodium	8.3mg
Carbohydrates	74.5g
Protein	2.6g

Ingredients

3 large ripe mangoes, peeled and seeded
1/2 C. sugar
2 tbsp lime juice
2 1/2 C. water
1 C. lemon juice

Directions

1. In a food processor, add the sugar and mangoes and pulse until smooth.
2. Transfer the pureed mango mixture into a pitcher.
3. Add the lemon juice and water and stir to combined.
4. Enjoy chilled.

3-INGREDIENT
Lemonade-Tea

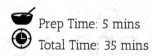

Prep Time: 5 mins
Total Time: 35 mins

Servings per Recipe: 8
Calories   8.7
Fat   0.0g
Cholesterol   0.0mg
Sodium   5.5mg
Carbohydrates   2.1g
Protein   0.0g

Ingredients

5 bags tea
1 quart water
1 C. sweetened strawberry-lemonade drink mix

Directions

1. In a pan, add the water and tea bags and cook until boiling.
2. Keep aside for about 35-40 minutes.
3. In a pitcher, add the tea and drink mix and mix until well combined.
4. Add enough cold water to fill the pitcher.
5. Enjoy.

New Lemonade Technology Tea

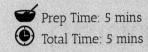

Prep Time: 5 mins
Total Time: 5 mins

Servings per Recipe: 8
Calories	70.8
Fat	0.1g
Cholesterol	0.0mg
Sodium	7.9mg
Carbohydrates	17.8g
Protein	0.0g

Ingredients

- 4 C. brewed tea
- 3 C. water
- 1 (6 oz.) cans frozen lemonade, thawed
- 1/4 C. sugar
- 1 tsp almond extract

Directions

1. In a pitcher, add all the ingredients and stir until well combined.
2. Transfer into ice filled glasses and enjoy.

LEMONADE
Tunisian

Prep Time: 5 mins
Total Time: 5 mins

Servings per Recipe: 6
Calories 120.8
Fat 0.2g
Cholesterol 0.0mg
Sodium 2.9mg
Carbohydrates 32.5g
Protein 0.9g

Ingredients

8 lemons, juiced
3/4 C. sugar
1 tsp orange blossom water
1/4 C. chopped mint

water
ice cube

Directions

1. In a pitcher, add the lemon juice and sugar and stir until dissolved.
2. Add the mint and orange blossom water and stir to combine well.
3. Divide the lemonade into serving glasses and fill with the ice and water.
4. Enjoy.

French Lemonade

Prep Time: 10 mins
Total Time: 30 mins

Servings per Recipe: 4	
Calories	208.7
Fat	0.0g
Cholesterol	0.0mg
Sodium	6.5mg
Carbohydrates	55.2g
Protein	0.2g

Ingredients

- 1 C. sugar
- 5 C. water, divided
- 1 tbsp dried lavender
- 1 C. fresh-squeezed lemon juice

Directions

1. In a pot, add the 2 C. of the water and sugar and cook until boiling, stirring continuously.
2. Add the lavender and stir to combine.
3. Remove from the heat and keep aside, covered for about 1-2 hours.
4. Through a strain, strain the mixture into a pitcher.
5. Add remaining 2 C. of the water and lemon juice and mix well.
6. Transfer into ice filled glasses and enjoy with the garnishing of the fresh lavender flowers.

COLLEGE
Lemonade

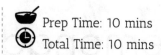
Prep Time: 10 mins
Total Time: 10 mins

Servings per Recipe: 8
Calories	169.5
Fat	0.2g
Cholesterol	0.0mg
Sodium	6.5mg
Carbohydrates	43.7g
Protein	0.2g

Ingredients

1 1/4 C. lemon juice
3/4 C. sugar
6 C. apple juice, unsweetened
1 C. water

Directions

1. In a food processor, add the sugar, 1/2 C. of the apple juice and lemon juice and pulse until well combined.
2. Keep aside or about 8-10 minutes.
3. Now, pulse for about 30-40 seconds.
4. Add 2 C. apple juice and the ice and pulse on low until well combined.
5. In a pitcher, place the mixture with the remaining apple juice and mix well.
6. Enjoy.

Cupcakes -Limon

Prep Time: 10 mins
Total Time: 35 mins

Servings per Recipe: 10	
Calories	332.2
Fat	17.1g
Cholesterol	32.8mg
Sodium	102.6mg
Carbohydrates	43.4g
Protein	2.4g

Ingredients

Cakes
1 C. all-purpose flour
1/2 tsp baking powder
1/4 tsp baking soda
1 pinch salt
1/2 C. granulated sugar
1/4 C. canola oil
2 egg whites
1/3 C. frozen pink lemonade concentrate, thawed
1/4 C. buttermilk
3 drops red food coloring
Frosting
1 1/2 C. icing sugar, sifted to remove lumps
1/2 C. unsalted butter
1 pinch salt
1/4 C. whipping cream
2 tsp frozen pink lemonade concentrate, thawed
1 tsp lemon extract
3 drops red food coloring

Directions

1. Set your oven to 375 degrees F before doing anything else and line 10 cups of a muffin pan with the paper liners.
2. In a bowl, add the flour, baking soda, baking powder and salt and mix well
3. In another bowl, add the lemonade concentrate, oil, sugar and egg whites and beat until smooth.
4. Add the flour mixture in three additions alternately with the buttermilk and beat until just combined.
5. Add the food coloring and stir to combine.
6. Transfer the mixture into the prepared muffin cups evenly.
7. Cook in the oven for about 20-25 minutes or until a toothpick inserted in the center comes out clean.
8. Remove from the oven and keep onto the wire rack to cool in the pan for about 5-10 minutes.

9. Carefully, invert the cupcakes onto the wire rack to cool completely.
10. Meanwhile, for the frosting: in a bowl, add the butter, sugar and salt and with an electric mixer, beat on low speed until creamy.
11. Now, beat on high speed until fluffy.
12. Add the lemon extract and lemonade concentrate and beat until well combined.
13. Add the cream and beat until fluffy.
14. Spread the frosting over the cooled cupcakes and enjoy.

Lemonade Levantine

Prep Time: 15 mins
Total Time: 1 hr 15 mins

Servings per Recipe: 6
Calories   143.4
Fat   0.2g
Cholesterol   0.0mg
Sodium   6.9mg
Carbohydrates   41.0g
Protein   0.8g

Ingredients

4 large fresh lemons, juiced
1 C. white sugar substitute
6 C. water

2 fresh oranges, juice, squeezed
1 tbsp orange blossom water

Directions

1. In a pitcher, add all the ingredients and mix until well combined..
2. Transfer into ice filled glasses and enjoy.

RIO DE JANEIRO
Restaurant Lemonade

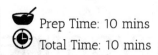

Prep Time: 10 mins
Total Time: 10 mins

Servings per Recipe: 4
Calories 114.1
Fat 0.4g
Cholesterol 1.6mg
Sodium 11.8mg
Carbohydrates 29.0g
Protein 0.6g

Ingredients

2 limes, wedges
1/2 C. sugar
3 tbsp milk, sweetened condensed
3 C. water
ice

Directions

1. In a food processor, add the sugar, limes, water, condensed milk and ice and pulse until smooth.
2. Through a sieve, strain the mixture, pressing with the back of a spoon.
3. Transfer into ice filled glasses and enjoy.

Heirloom Kitchen Lemonade

Prep Time: 10 mins
Total Time: 11 mins

Servings per Recipe: 6
Calories   150.4
Fat   0.1g
Cholesterol   0.0mg
Sodium   6.3mg
Carbohydrates   38.9g
Protein   0.3g

Ingredients

1 C. unbleached white sugar
1/2 C. filtered water
1 tbsp grated ginger
1 tbsp chopped fresh grown lemon verbena plant leaves

1 C. blueberries
1/2 C. fresh lemon juice
4 C. filtered water

Directions

1. In a pan, add the lemon verbena, ginger, 1/2 C. of the sugar and 1/2 C. of the water and cook for about 2 minutes, stirring continuously.
2. Remove from the heat and place the sugar syrup into a container.
3. Refrigerate, covered to chill before using.
4. In a food processor, add the remaining 1/2 C. of the sugar and blueberries and pulse until smooth.
5. Add the remaining water and lemon juice and pulse until well combined.
6. In a bowl, add the chilled syrup and blueberry mixture and mix well.
7. Through a strainer, strain the mixture into a pitcher.
8. Transfer into ice filled glasses and enjoy with the whole fresh lemon verbena leaves.

SUMMER Solstice Lemonade

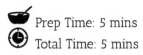

Prep Time: 5 mins
Total Time: 5 mins

Servings per Recipe: 1
Calories   81.1
Fat   1.0g
Cholesterol   0.0mg
Sodium   1.5mg
Carbohydrates   18.6g
Protein   1.8g

Ingredients

lemonade
1 pint fresh raspberry
1 bunch fresh mint leaves

Directions

1. In each section of an ice cube tray, put 1 mint leaf and 1 raspberry.
2. now, add enough lemonade in each section to fill it.
3. Place the ice cube tray in freezer until set completely.
4. Fill ice cube tray with lemonade and freeze until set.
5. After freezing, add the cubes in lemonade.

Lemonade Madras

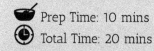

Prep Time: 10 mins
Total Time: 20 mins

Servings per Recipe: 10
Calories   66.7
Fat   0.1g
Cholesterol   0.0mg
Sodium   241.5mg
Carbohydrates   18.2g
Protein   0.5g

Ingredients

11 C. water (divided)
2/3 C. sugar
9 -10 lemons, juiced

1 tsp salt

Directions

1. For the sugar syrup: in a pan, add the sugar and 1 C. of the water and cook until sugar is dissolved, stirring continuously.
2. Remove from the heat and keep aside to cool completely.
3. Through a fine mesh strainer, strain the seeds from the lemon juice and keep aside.
4. In a pitcher, add the lemon juice, cooled sugar syrup, 1 tsp of salt and 10 C. of the cold water and stir to combine.
5. Transfer into ice filled glasses and enjoy

LEMONADE in France (Citron Presse)

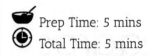

Prep Time: 5 mins
Total Time: 5 mins

Servings per Recipe: 1
Calories 1548.0
Fat 0.0g
Cholesterol 0.0mg
Sodium 18.2mg
Carbohydrates 399.9g
Protein 0.0g

Ingredients

2 C. sugar
peel from 2 lemon, julienned
2 C. water

mint sprig
juice of half a lemon

Directions

1. For the lemon syrup: in a pot, add the lemon, sugar and water and cook until boiling.
2. Cook for about 5 minutes.
3. Remove from the heat and keep aside to cool.
4. Transfer the syrup into a glass jar and place in the fridge until using.
5. In a serving glass, place 1 tbsp of the lemon syrup, lemon juice, mint sprig and a few ice cubes.
6. Add enough cold water and stir to combine.
7. Enjoy.

Lena's Lemonade

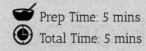

Prep Time: 5 mins
Total Time: 5 mins

Servings per Recipe: 1
Calories	112.1
Fat	0.1g
Cholesterol	0.0mg
Sodium	5.2mg
Carbohydrates	29.1g
Protein	0.1g

Ingredients

- 2 tbsp fresh squeezed lemon juice
- 2 tbsp Maple syrup
- 1/4 tbsp Cayenne Pepper
- 1 C. of purified distilled water

Directions

1. In a pitcher, add all the ingredients and mix well.
2. Enjoy.

LEMONADE in France (Citron Presse)

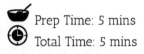
Prep Time: 5 mins
Total Time: 5 mins

Servings per Recipe: 1
Calories   1548.0
Fat   0.0g
Cholesterol   0.0mg
Sodium   18.2mg
Carbohydrates   399.9g
Protein   0.0g

Ingredients

2 C. sugar
peel from 2 lemon, julienned
2 C. water

mint sprig
juice of half a lemon

Directions

1. For the lemon syrup: in a pot, add the lemon, sugar and water and cook until boiling.
2. Cook for about 5 minutes.
3. Remove from the heat and keep aside to cool.
4. Transfer the syrup into a glass jar and place in the fridge until using.
5. In a serving glass, place 1 tbsp of the lemon syrup, lemon juice, mint sprig and a few ice cubes.
6. Add enough cold water and stir to combine.
7. Enjoy.

Mexican Lemonade

Prep Time: 10 mins
Total Time: 12 mins

Servings per Recipe: 1
Calories   865.5
Fat   0.0g
Cholesterol   0.0mg
Sodium   13.1mg
Carbohydrates   231.5g
Protein   1.3g

Ingredients

4 C. water, divided
2 C. sugar
1 vanilla bean, split

3 C. fresh lemon juice

Directions

1. In a pot, add sugar, vanilla bean and 2 C. of the water over medium-high heat and cook until boiling.
2. Cook for about 1 minute.
3. Remove from the heat and keep aside to cool completely.
4. Add 2 C. of the water and lemon juice and mix well.
5. Place in fridge to chill completely.
6. Transfer into ice filled glasses and enjoy with a garnishing of the maraschino cherries, lemon slices and fresh mint.

LEMONADE
for Lovers

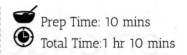

Prep Time: 10 mins
Total Time: 1 hr 10 mins

Servings per Recipe: 5
Calories	165.5
Fat	0.1g
Cholesterol	0.0mg
Sodium	6.5mg
Carbohydrates	43.3g
Protein	0.1

Ingredients

4 C. water
1/4 C. organic fresh edible lavender, well rinsed
1 fresh lemon, zest
1 C. fresh lemon juice
1 C. sugar
lemon slice

Directions

1. In a pan, add 1 C. of the water and cook until boiling.
2. Stir in the lemon zest and lavender and remove from the heat.
3. Keep aside, covered for about 60-70 minutes.
4. Through a strainer, strain the lavender mixture into a pitcher.
5. Add the sugar, lemon juice and remaining 3 C. of the water and mix until sugar is dissolved completely.
6. Transfer into ice filled glasses and enjoy with a garnishing of the lemon slices.
7. You can enjoy this tea hot with honey.

Lunch Truck Lemonade

Prep Time: 3 mins
Total Time: 13 mins

Servings per Recipe: 8
Calories 134.5
Fat 0.0g
Cholesterol 0.0mg
Sodium 7.2mg
Carbohydrates 36.8g
Protein 0.2g

Ingredients

- 1 C. honey
- 1 C. hot water
- 3/4 C. lemon juice
- 8 C. cold water

Directions

1. In a pan, add the hot water and honey over low heat and cook until well combined.
2. Remove from the heat and keep aside to cool completely.
3. Stir in the cold water and lemon juice.
4. Transfer into ice filled glasses and enjoy.

RED
Lemonade

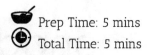

Prep Time: 5 mins
Total Time: 5 mins

Servings per Recipe:	1
Calories	167.0
Fat	0.0g
Cholesterol	0.0mg
Sodium	15.7mg
Carbohydrates	46.5g
Protein	0.6g

Ingredients

6 oz. lemon juice, fresh squeezed
4 tbsp confectioners' sugar
24 oz. water
4 oz. cherry juice concentrate

Directions

1. In a pitcher, add the sugar and lemon juice and mix until sugar is dissolved completely.
2. Add the cherry juice concentrate and water and mix well.
3. Transfer into ice filled glasses and enjoy.

Lemonade Icee's

Prep Time: 15 mins
Total Time: 8 hrs 15 mins

Servings per Recipe: 1	
Calories	551.9
Fat	1.5g
Cholesterol	0.0mg
Sodium	16.1mg
Carbohydrates	143.9g
Protein	2.7g

Ingredients

- 2 C. lemon juice
- 1 1/2 C. fresh raspberries
- 1 1/2 C. fresh blueberries
- 1 C. sugar
- 3 C. cold water

Directions

1. In a food processor, add the sugar, both berries and lemon juice and pulse until smooth.
2. Through a fine mesh strainer, strain the mixture by pressing with the back of a wooden spoon.
3. In a pitcher, add the water and berry mixture and mix well.
4. Now, transfer the mixture into a container.
5. Seal the container and place in the freezer for all the night.
6. Remove from the freezer and keep aside in room temperature for about 45 minutes.
7. Enjoy.

ARIZONA
Mesa Lemonade

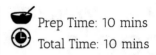

Prep Time: 10 mins
Total Time: 10 mins

Servings per Recipe: 1
Calories	548.6
Fat	1.2g
Cholesterol	0.0mg
Sodium	30.4mg
Carbohydrates	143.8g
Protein	2.6g

Ingredients

1/2 C. sugar
1/2 C. water
1/2 C. lightly packed mint leaves
1 C. fresh lemon juice
1 1/2 C. cold water
6 oz. blueberries
1 C. ice cube
seltzer water

Directions

1. In a pan, add the mint, sugar and water and cook until boiling, mixing continuously.
2. Cook until a syrup is formed.
3. Remove from the heat and keep aside to cool.
4. Through a strainer, strain the syrup into a pitcher.
5. Add the water and lemon juice and mix well.
6. Divide blueberries and ice cubes in serving glasses.
7. Pour lemonade and seltzer water and enjoy.

Rachela's Sweet Lemonade with Vegetable Syrup

Prep Time: 5 mins
Total Time: 15 mins

Servings per Recipe: 10
Calories   59.7
Fat   0.0g
Cholesterol   0.0mg
Sodium   0.9mg
Carbohydrates   15.5g
Protein   0.0g

Ingredients

Vegetable Syrup:
2 large stalk rhubarb, chopped
1/4 C. lemon juice
1 large lemon, zest
3/4 C. sugar
1 C. water

Lemonade:
1 part rhubarb lemon syrup
2 parts water
ice

Directions

1. For the rhubarb syrup: in a pot, add the sugar, rhubarb, lemon zest, lemon juice and water over medium heat and cook for about 11-12 minutes.
2. Through a strainer, strain the mixture into a pitcher and refrigerate to chill.
3. In each ice filled serving glass, place 1 portion of the cooled syrup and 2 portions of the water and mix well.
4. Enjoy.

GREEK
Lemonade

Prep Time: 10 mins
Total Time: 15 mins

Servings per Recipe: 24
Calories   44.1
Fat   0.1g
Cholesterol   0.0mg
Sodium   2.9mg
Carbohydrates   11.2g
Protein   0.0g

Ingredients

3 tbsp fresh rosemary, chopped
1/4 C. sugar
1 C. water
1 (12 oz.) cans frozen lemonade concentrate, thawed

3 (12 oz.) cans water

Directions

1. In a pan, add the sugar, rosemary and 1 C. of the water over medium heat and cook until boiling.
2. Cook for about 5 minutes.
3. Through a strainer, strain the mixture into a bowl.
4. Let the mixture cool completely.
5. In a pitcher, add the cooled rosemary mixture, lemonade concentrate and water and mix well.
6. Transfer into ice filled glasses and enjoy with a garnishing of the fresh rosemary sprigs.

Festival Lemonade

Prep Time: 15 mins
Total Time: 17 mins

Servings per Recipe: 1
Calories   827.6
Fat   0.5g
Cholesterol   0.0mg
Sodium   11.5mg
Carbohydrates   216.8g
Protein   0.8g

Ingredients

- 1 C. water
- 1 C. sugar
- 10 rose-scented geranium leaves
- 1 C. lemon juice
- chilled water

Directions

1. In a pan, add the sugar and water and cook until boiling.
2. Remove from the heat and stir in the geranium leaves.
3. Keep aside, covered for whole night.
4. Squeeze the geranium leaves twice.
5. Stir in the lemon and transfer the mixture into bottle.
6. Place in the fridge to cool.
7. In each ice filled serving glass, add 1 tbsp of the concentrate and 1 C. of the chilled water and stir to combine.
8. Enjoy with a garnishing of the scented geranium leaves.

VIETNAMESE
Lemonade

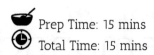
Prep Time: 15 mins
Total Time: 15 mins

Servings per Recipe: 4
Calories	633.9
Fat	0.0g
Cholesterol	0.0mg
Sodium	5.3mg
Carbohydrates	164.1g
Protein	0.0g

Ingredients

Syrup:
1 liter water
650 g sugar
Lemonade:
160 ml simple syrup
6 lime slices
8 sprigs of fresh mint
4 sprigs of fresh mint
80 ml fresh squeezed lime juice
sparkling water

Directions

1. For the simple syrup: in a pot, add the sugar and water and cook until boiling, mixing continuously.
2. Cook until the sugar dissolves completely.
3. Remove from the heat and keep aside to cool.
4. Place 2 mint sprigs and 1 lime slice in each serving glass.
5. Now, place the simple syrup, lime juice and ice cubes in each glass and mix well.
6. Add enough sparkling water to fill each glass and enjoy with a garnishing of the remaining mint sprigs.

Israeli Style Lemonade

Prep Time: 30 mins
Total Time: 30 mins

Servings per Recipe: 6
Calories   212.0
Fat   0.0g
Cholesterol   0.0mg
Sodium   3.0mg
Carbohydrates   59.2g
Protein   0.7g

Ingredients

1 1/4 C. water
1 1/4 C. sugar
1/4 C. lemon verbena leaf
5 C. fresh lemon juice, strained

Flavored Ice
boiled water, cooled
24 lemon verbena leaves

Directions

1. For the verbena ice cubes: fill each section of 2 ice cube trays with enough water to come halfway through.
2. Place in the freezer until set.
3. Now, place 1 lemon verbena leaf over each cube and pour water to fill the each section completely.
4. Place in the freezer for up to 6-7 days.
5. In a pot, add the sugar and 4 C. of the water and cook until boiling.
6. Cook until the sugar dissolves completely.
7. Remove from the heat and stir in the lemon verbena.
8. Keep aside, covered for about 20 minutes.
9. Through a fine mesh strainer, strain the mixture into a bowl and keep aside to cool.
10. In a pitcher, add the lemon verbena syrup and lemon juice and mix well.
11. Fill each serving glass with lemon verbena ice cubes.
12. Pour the lemonade and enjoy.

OCTOBER
Cinnamon Clove Lemonade

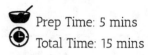

Prep Time: 5 mins
Total Time: 15 mins

Servings per Recipe: 1	
Calories	333.9
Fat	0.2g
Cholesterol	0.0mg
Sodium	17.4mg
Carbohydrates	92.1g
Protein	1.2g

Ingredients

6 C. water, divided
3/4 C. sugar
2 cinnamon sticks
6 whole cloves
1 large lime, sliced
1 lemon, sliced

3/4 C. fresh lemon juice

Directions

1. In a pot, add the sugar, cloves, cinnamon sticks and 4 C. of the water and cook until boiling.
2. Set the heat to low and cook for about 9 minutes.
3. Remove from the heat and remove the cloves and cinnamon sticks.
4. Keep side to cool completely.
5. In a pitcher, add the lemon, lime slices, lemon juice, sugar syrup and remaining water and mix well.
6. Refrigerate for about 2 hours.
7. Enjoy chilled.

Tarrytown Lemonade

Prep Time: 5 mins
Total Time: 30 mins

Servings per Recipe: 12
Calories   177.6
Fat   0.0g
Cholesterol   0.0mg
Sodium   5.3mg
Carbohydrates   48.6g
Protein   0.5g

Ingredients

- 10 C. water
- 2 1/4 C. sugar
- 17 sprigs fresh tarragon
- 6 C. fresh lemon juice
- 12 lemon slices
- salt
- ice

Directions

1. In a pot, add the sugar and 4 C. of water over medium-high heat and cook until boiling, mixing continuously.
2. Cook for about 26 minutes, stirring occasionally.
3. Remove from the heat and stir in 5 tarragon sprigs.
4. Keep aside for about 28 minutes, mixing occasionally.
5. Remove the tarragon sprigs.
6. In a large pitcher, add the tarragon syrup, lemon juice, remaining water and pinch of salt and mix well.
7. Transfer into ice filled glasses and enjoy with a garnishing of the remaining tarragon sprigs and lemon slices.

SANIBEL ISLAND
Lemonade

Prep Time: 15 mins
Total Time: 25 mins

Servings per Recipe: 8
Calories	72.0
Fat	0.0g
Cholesterol	0.0mg
Sodium	1.3mg
Carbohydrates	20.0g
Protein	0.1g

Ingredients

- 1 C. fresh lemon juice
- 1/2 C. honey
- 6 C. sparkling water
- 1 lemon, zest
- coarse salt
- lemon wedges

Directions

1. In a pan, add the honey and lemon juice and cook until well combined.
2. Remove from the heat and keep aide to cool.
3. Transfer into a bowl and refrigerate to chill.
4. In a pitcher, add the honey syrup and sparkling water and mix well.
5. In a shallow dish mix together the coarse salt and lemon zest.
6. Massage a lemon wedge over the rim of each serving glass evenly.
7. Now, coat the rim of each glass with salt mixture.
8. Pour the lemonade and ice in each glass and enjoy.

Hawaiian Lemonade

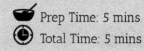

Prep Time: 5 mins
Total Time: 5 mins

Servings per Recipe: 1
Calories	104.7
Fat	0.1g
Cholesterol	0.0mg
Sodium	6.0mg
Carbohydrates	25.3g
Protein	0.7g

Ingredients

1 (12 oz.) cans frozen lemonade concentrate, thawed
1 (12 oz.) cans frozen orange juice concentrate, thawed
1 (64 oz.) cans pineapple juice
1 gallon water
1 tbsp vanilla
1 tbsp almond extract

Directions

1. In a pitcher, add all the ingredients and mix well.
2. Transfer into ice filled glasses and enjoy.

LEMONADE
Lake

Prep Time: 15 mins
Total Time: 25 mins

Servings per Recipe: 1
Calories   115.9
Fat   0.2g
Cholesterol   0.0mg
Sodium   4.2mg
Carbohydrates   30.6g
Protein   0.6g

Ingredients

3 C. blueberries
1 C. fresh lemon juice, reserving the rind
1/2 C. sugar

4 C. water
1 - 1 1/2 tsp lavender flowers

Directions

1. In a glass bowl, add the blueberries and with the back of a wooden spoon, crush them lightly.
2. Add the sugar and lemon juice and mix well.
3. In a pot, add the lavender buds and 4 C. of the water and cook until boiling.
4. Through a fine mesh strainer, strain the mixture into the bowl of blueberries.
5. Stir in the lemon rinds and place in the fridge for about 3 hour.
6. Discard the lemon rinds.
7. Through a fine mesh strainer, strain the mixture into a strainer.
8. Transfer into ice filled glasses and enjoy.

Root Lemonade

Prep Time: 5 mins
Total Time: 40 mins

Servings per Recipe: 12
Calories   41.2
Fat   0.1g
Cholesterol   0.0mg
Sodium   2.1mg
Carbohydrates   13.1g
Protein   0.5g

Ingredients

- 2 C. water
- 1/2 C. sugar
- 1 inch piece ginger root, peeled and sliced
- 5 lemons, halved
- 2 C. apple cider

Directions

1. In a pot, add the ginger, sugar and water and cook until boiling.
2. Cook for about 1 minute.
3. Remove from the heat and stir in the lemons.
4. Keep aside for about 30 minutes.
5. Carefully, squeeze the lemons to extract the juice.
6. Through a fine mesh strainer, strain the lemon mixture into a bowl.
7. Add the cider and stir to combine.
8. Refrigerate for about 2 hours
9. Enjoy chilled.

LEMONADE
Pagani

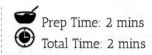

Prep Time: 2 mins
Total Time: 2 mins

Servings per Recipe: 4
Calories	120.1
Fat	0.0g
Cholesterol	0.0mg
Sodium	7.8mg
Carbohydrates	32.1g
Protein	0.3g

Ingredients

3 C. pear nectar, chilled
1/2 C. fresh lemon juice
1/3 C. Splenda granular, sugar substitute

4 tsp ginger juice

Directions

1. In a pitcher, add all the ingredients and mix until Splenda is dissolved.
2. Transfer into ice filled glasses and enjoy.

Leafy Lemonade

Prep Time: 5 mins
Total Time: 5 mins

Servings per Recipe: 2
Calories   56.3
Fat   0.0g
Cholesterol   0.0mg
Sodium   5.0mg
Carbohydrates   15.2g
Protein   0.1g

Ingredients

1/4 C. lemon juice, squeezed
2 tbsp sugar
4 leaves borage

2 C. water

Directions

1. In a food processor, add all the ingredients and pulse until well combined.
2. Through a strainer, strain the mixture into a pitcher.
3. Transfer into ice filled glasses and enjoy.

LONDON Lemonade Squares

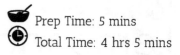

Prep Time: 5 mins
Total Time: 4 hrs 5 mins

Servings per Recipe: 9
Calories   267.6
Fat   11.7g
Cholesterol   1.2mg
Sodium   220.0mg
Carbohydrates   37.7g
Protein   3.6g

Ingredients

18 squares graham crackers, crushed
1/3 C. margarine
1 quart vanilla frozen yogurt

1 (6 oz.) cans frozen lemonade concentrate

Directions

1. For the crust: in a bowl, add the margarine and graham cracker crumbs and mix well.
2. In the bottom of 9-inch square pan, pace the crumb mixture and with your hands, press to smooth the surface.
3. In a bowl, add the lemonade concentrate and yogurt and with an electric mixer, beat until smooth.
4. Place the lemonade mixture over the crust evenly.
5. Place in the freezer for about 5 hours.
6. Cut into desired sized squares and enjoy.

Canadian Mexican Lemonade

Prep Time: 5 mins
Total Time: 5 mins

Servings per Recipe: 1
Calories   150.3
Fat   0.1g
Cholesterol   0.0mg
Sodium   8.4mg
Carbohydrates   39.5g
Protein   0.1g

Ingredients

1 C. fresh lemon juice
1 C. pure maple syrup
4 C. water
1/8-1/4 tsp ground red pepper 2 C. water

Directions

1. In a pitcher, add all the ingredients and mix well.
2. Transfer into ice filled glasses and enjoy.

ROSEMARY
Honey Lemonade

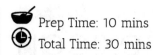

Prep Time: 10 mins
Total Time: 30 mins

Servings per Recipe: 4
Calories 95.2
Fat 0.4g
Cholesterol 0.0mg
Sodium 9.5mg
Carbohydrates 25.5g
Protein 0.9g

Ingredients

1 quart boiling water
1/4 C. fresh rosemary leaves
3 medium lemons
1/4-1/2 C. honey
1 C. fresh raspberries

ice cube
fresh edible flower

Directions

1. For the rosemary infusion: in a heat-proof bowl, add the rosemary and boiling water.
2. Keep aside for about 18-20 minutes
3. Through a strainer, strain t into a bowl.
4. Add the fresh lemon and honey and mix well.
5. Transfer into glasses with the ice cubes and raspberries.
6. Enjoy with a garnishing of the edible flowers.

Mother's Day Lemonade

Prep Time: 10 mins
Total Time: 15 mins

Servings per Recipe: 1
Calories	2215.7
Fat	0.0g
Cholesterol	0.0mg
Sodium	22.3mg
Carbohydrates	592.2g
Protein	2.8g

Ingredients

- 2 C. sugar
- 1/2 C. honey
- 2 C. water
- 1 vanilla bean
- 2 1/2 C. fresh lemon juice
- lemon slice
- water

Directions

1. Split the vanilla bean in half lengthwise.
2. With the back of a knife, scratch the vanilla seeds.
3. In a pot, add the honey, sugar, vanilla seeds with pod and 2 C. of the water over medium-high heat and cook until boiling.
4. Cook for about 3-5 minutes, stirring frequently.
5. Remove from the heat and keep aside to cool completely.
6. Through a strainer, strain the sugar syrup into a pitcher.
7. Add the lemon juice and enough water to have 1 gallon of the drink and mix well.
8. Transfer into ice filled glasses and enjoy with a garnishing of the lemon slices.

LEMONADE
in Vietcong

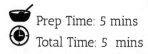
Prep Time: 5 mins
Total Time: 5 mins

Servings per Recipe: 10
Calories 53.1
Fat 0.0g
Cholesterol 0.0mg
Sodium 1.4mg
Carbohydrates 15.4g
Protein 0.3g

Ingredients

110 g caster sugar
1/2 C. ice
250 ml fresh lemon juice
2 lemons, sliced
1 bunch mint leaf

2 1/2 liters mineral water

Directions

1. In a pitcher, add all the ingredients and stir to combine well.
2. Enjoy in tall glasses.

Sweet Basil Lemonade

Prep Time: 10 mins
Total Time: 15 mins

Servings per Recipe: 1
Calories   128.1
Fat   0.2g
Cholesterol   0.0mg
Sodium   5.0mg
Carbohydrates   32.9g
Protein   0.8g

Ingredients

3 1/2 C. water
1 C. fresh basil leaf, plus additional fresh basil leaf
2 nectarines, chopped
3/4 C. sugar
1 C. fresh lemon juice

Directions

1. In a pot, add the sugar, 1 nectarine, 1 C. of the basil and 2 C. of the water and cook until boiling, mixing continuously.
2. Cook for about 5 minutes.
3. Remove from the heat and keep aside to cool completely.
4. Through a fine mesh strainer, strain the mixture into a pitcher, pressing with the back of a spoon.
5. Add the remaining sliced nectarines, lemon juice and 1 1/2 C. of the water and stir to combine
6. Transfer into ice filled glasses and enjoy with a garnishing of the extra basil.

LEMONADE
Monday Muffins

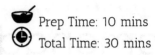
Prep Time: 10 mins
Total Time: 30 mins

Servings per Recipe: 12
Calories 206.5
Fat 6.2g
Cholesterol 31.6mg
Sodium 235.6mg
Carbohydrates 34.9g
Protein 3.3g

Ingredients

2 C. flour
9 tbsp sugar, divided
4 tsp poppy seeds
3 tsp baking powder
1/2 tsp salt

3/4 C. lemonade concentrate, divided
1/2 C. low-fat milk
1/3 C. butter, melted
1 egg

Directions

1. Set your oven to 350 degrees F before doing anything else and line 12 cups of a muffin pan with the paper liners.
2. Add the flour, poppy seeds, 5 tbsp of the sugar, baking powder and salt in a bowl and mix well.
3. In a separate bowl, add the eggs, milk, butter and 1/2 C. of the lemonade concentrate and beat until well combined.
4. Add the flour mixture and mix until just combined.
5. Place the mixture into the prepared muffin cups about 3/4 of the full.
6. Cook in the oven for about 15-20 minutes or until a toothpick inserted in the center comes out clean.
7. Remove from the oven and keep onto the wire rack to cool in the pan for about 5 minutes.
8. Carefully, invert the muffins onto the wire rack.
9. Meanwhile, for the glaze: in a bowl, add the remaining lemonade concentrate and sugar and mix well.
10. With a fork, poke ye top of each muffin at many places.
11. Place the lemonade mixture over each muffin and enjoy.

Dade County Lemonade

Prep Time: 30 mins
Total Time: 31 mins

Servings per Recipe: 4
Calories   121.9
Fat   0.2g
Cholesterol   0.0mg
Sodium   17.9mg
Carbohydrates   33.1g
Protein   0.9g

Ingredients

7 tea bags
1/2 C. white sugar
5 C. water
4 -5 C. ice cubes

6 lemons, squeezed
3 sprigs mint

Directions

1. In a pot, add the water and cook until boiling.
2. Add the sugar and stir until dissolve completely.
3. Add the mint and teabags and mint and cook until boiling.
4. Remove from the heat and keep aside, covered for about 8-10 minutes.
5. Remove the mint and tea bags and discard them.
6. Stir in the lemon juice.
7. Transfer into ice filled glasses and enjoy.

HOW TO MAKE
Lemonade Syrup

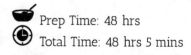

Prep Time: 48 hrs
Total Time: 48 hrs 5 mins

Servings per Recipe: 1
Calories   881.5
Fat   0.1g
Cholesterol   0.0mg
Sodium   7.5mg
Carbohydrates   230.7g
Protein   0.6g

Ingredients

450 g caster sugar
600 ml water
1 lemon, cut into two halves
10 large lemon verbena leaves
10 large lemon balm leaves
1/4 tsp tartaric

Directions

1. In a pot, add the lemon halves, sugar and water and Cook until sugar dissolves completely, stirring frequently.
2. Stir in the lemon balm leaves and lemon verbena and cook for about 3 minutes.
3. Remove from the heat and keep aside to cool completely.
4. Stir in the tartaric acid and keep aside, covered for 28-45 hours.
5. Through a strainer, strain the mixture.
6. Now, transfer the mixture into sterile bottles.
7. Seal the bottles tightly and preserve in a cool dark area for 2-3 months.
8. In serving glasses, add 1 portion of the syrup with 4 portions of the water and enjoy with a garnishing of lemon verbena leaves.

Cucumber Lemonade

Prep Time: 5 mins
Total Time: 5 mins

Servings per Recipe: 2
Calories   119.5
Fat   1.1g
Cholesterol   0.0mg
Sodium   48.5mg
Carbohydrates   30.8g
Protein   5.1g

Ingredients

1 bunch kale
1 cucumber
1 lemon

1 granny smith apple

Directions

1. In a juicer, add all the ingredients and extract the juice according to manufacturer's instructions.
2. Transfer into ice filled glasses and enjoy.

TODDLER'S
Lemonade

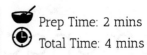

Prep Time: 2 mins
Total Time: 4 mins

Servings per Recipe: 2
Calories 158.5
Fat 0.4g
Cholesterol 0.0mg
Sodium 6.3mg
Carbohydrates 41.1g
Protein 1.3g

Ingredients

2 ripe bananas, peeled
1 pint cold water
1 lime, juice

2 - 4 tbsp sugar
ice

Directions

1. In a microwave-safe bowl, add the banana and microwave on high for about 40-60 seconds.
2. In a food processor, add the hot bananas and remaining ingredients and pulse until smooth.
3. Through a strainer, strain the mixture into a pitcher.
4. Transfer into ice filled glasses and enjoy.

Hawaiian Tribal Lemonade

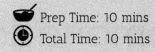

Prep Time: 10 mins
Total Time: 10 mins

Servings per Recipe: 5
Calories 162.8
Fat 0.2g
Cholesterol 0.0mg
Sodium 6.5mg
Carbohydrates 43.5g
Protein 0.5g

Ingredients

1 (20 oz.) cans lychees in heavy syrup
1 (12 oz.) cans frozen lemonade concentrate
2 1/2 C. water
ice cube
1 lemon, sliced
5 sprigs mint

Directions

1. In a food processor, add the lemonade concentrate, lychees with syrup and water and pulse until smooth.
2. Transfer into ice filled glasses and enjoy with a garnishing of the lemon slices and mint sprigs.

STATE FAIR
Lemonade

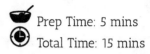

Prep Time: 5 mins
Total Time: 15 mins

Servings per Recipe: 1
Calories	172.7
Fat	0.2g
Cholesterol	0.0mg
Sodium	10.7mg
Carbohydrates	45.5g
Protein	0.4g

Ingredients

1 1/2 C. lemon juice, seeds and pith removed
1 C. sugar
4 C. cold water
2 lemons, sliced

ice
5 C. pink cotton candy

Directions

1. In a pitcher, add the sugar and lemon juice and mix until dissolves completely.
2. Stir in the lemon slices and cold water and continue stirring until well combined.
3. Divide the lemonade and ice into serving glasses.
4. Add the cotton candy and stir until dissolves completely.
5. Enjoy.

Urban Garden Lemonade

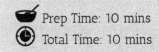
Prep Time: 10 mins
Total Time: 10 mins

Servings per Recipe: 8
Calories	16.9
Fat	0.1g
Cholesterol	0.0mg
Sodium	2.2mg
Carbohydrates	4.1g
Protein	0.7g

Ingredients

3 - 4 cucumbers, peeled and chopped
8 - 10 mint leaves
1 lemonade
ice cube

Directions

1. In a food processor, add the cucumbers and mint and pulse until smooth.
2. Through a fine mesh strainer, strain the mixture into a bowl, pressing with the back of a wooden spoon.
3. In a pitcher, add the lemonade, cucumber mixture and ice cubes and mix well.
4. Enjoy chilled.

LEMONADE
Saint Kitts

🥣 Prep Time: 10 mins
🕐 Total Time: 2 hrs 10 mins

Servings per Recipe: 4
Calories   129.0
Fat   0.3g
Cholesterol   0.0mg
Sodium   6.6mg
Carbohydrates   33.1g
Protein   0.5g

Ingredients

3 C. warm water
2/3 C. lemon juice
1/2 C. sugar
2 tbsp coconut syrup
1/2 C. unsweetened frozen blueberries
1/2 C. frozen red raspberries
1 small star fruit, sliced
ice cube

Directions

1. In a bowl add the sugar, lemon juice, coconut syrup and water and mix until sugar dissolves completely.
2. Cover the bowl and place in the fridge for about 8-20 hours.
3. In a pitcher, add the lemon mixture, berries and star fruit slices and mix.
4. Transfer into ice filled glasses and enjoy.

Lebanese Lebanese Lemonade

Prep Time: 5 mins
Total Time: 5 mins

Servings per Recipe: 1
Calories   87.9
Fat   0.9g
Cholesterol   0.0mg
Sodium   47.6mg
Carbohydrates   25.9g
Protein   1.9g

Ingredients

- 1 whole organic lemon
- 1 C. squeezed lemon juice
- 1 C. agave nectar
- 1 tbsp of grated ginger
- mint leaves
- 6 - 8 C. of filtered water

Directions

1. In a pot, add the lemon juice and agave and cook until well combined.
2. Remove from the heat and keep aside to cool completely.
3. In a food processor, add the lemon, ginger and agave syrup and pulse until frothy.
4. Add the water and stir to combine.
5. Enjoy with a garnishing of the fresh mint leaves.

BLACK Lemonade

Prep Time: 30 mins
Total Time: 30 mins

Servings per Recipe: 1	
Calories	1297.5
Fat	1.2g
Cholesterol	0.0mg
Sodium	35.7mg
Carbohydrates	337.4g
Protein	2.5g

Ingredients

- 4 C. water
- 1 1/2 C. sugar
- 6 lemons, juice and zest
- 1/2 C. blackberry
- 1/2 C. blueberries

Directions

1. In a pan, add the sugar and 2 C. of the water and cook until sugar is dissolved, stirring continuously.
2. Cook for about 4 minutes, stirring frequently.
3. Remove from the heat and stir in the lemon juice, lemon zest and remaining water.
4. Keep aside to cool completely.
5. In a food processor, add both berries and pulse until smooth.
6. Add the berry puree into the lemonade and stir to combine.
7. Keep aside for about 3 hours.
8. Through a strainer, strain the lemonade into pitcher.
9. Refrigerate until chilled completely.
10. Enjoy chilled.

ENJOY THE RECIPES?
KEEP ON COOKING WITH 6 MORE FREE COOKBOOKS!

Visit our website and simply enter your email address to join the club and receive your 6 cookbooks.

http://booksumo.com/magnet

 https://www.instagram.com/booksumopress/

 https://www.facebook.com/booksumo/

CPSIA information can be obtained
at www.ICGtesting.com
Printed in the USA
LVHW102330071019
633403LV00008B/2707/P